MW00906485

# Penguins
## Facts About Penguins

A CHILDRENS WORLD BOOK COLLECTION

BARRY J MCDONALD

# COPYRIGHT

ALL RIGHTS RESERVED. No part of this book may be reproduced or transmitted in any form whatsoever, electronic, or mechanical, including photocopying, recording, or by any informational storage or retrieval system without express written, dated and signed permission from the author.

http://www.SmartWordBooks.com

Copyright © 2013 Published by Barry McDonald

# DID YOU KNOW...

Penguins have a special gland close to their tail that makes oil. This oil helps to keep their feathers water and wind proof.

Penguins don't seem to be afraid of humans and will happily approach them (up to 10 feet away) without any hesitation.

Penguins spend 3/4 of their lives in the ocean looking for food.

Penguins feed on fish, krill, squid and other small sea life when swimming in the ocean. But this can vary depending on the season and what type of foods that's available.

Compared to other birds, penguins have solid heavy bones which is why they're too heavy to fly.

In the sea a penguins enemies are the Orca whale, shark and leopard seal which like to catch penguins for food.

Although all penguins have more or less the same body shape they vary in size from 1kg in weight up to 40kgs.

When taking care of younger penguins, the older penguins form a circle around them to keep them safe from danger.

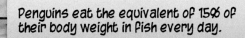

Penguins eat the equivalent of 15% of their body weight in fish every day.

In extremely harsh cold Emperor penguins can huddle in groups of up to 5000 to keep warm. Older and sick penguins stay close to the centre while younger, fitter penguins take turns standing on the outer

Emperor penguins are the largest of all penguins weighing up to 40kgs.

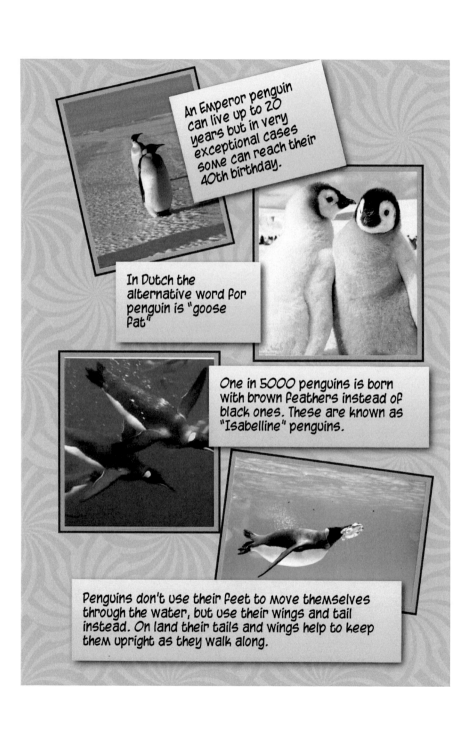

An Emperor penguin can live up to 20 years but in very exceptional cases some can reach their 40th birthday.

In Dutch the alternative word for penguin is "goose fat"

One in 5000 penguins is born with brown feathers instead of black ones. These are known as "Isabelline" penguins.

Penguins don't use their feet to move themselves through the water, but use their wings and tail instead. On land their tails and wings help to keep them upright as they walk along.

When penguins are in a hurry they slide on the ice using their bellies and feet. This is known as "Tobogganing".

No penguins live at the North Pole. Most penguins live in the Antarctic and Southern Hemisphere.

Penguins normally always stick to the same path when coming from and going to the ocean to bathe and feed.

Compared to other penguins Emperor penguins have smaller beaks and flippers to help conserve heat.

Emperor penguins never build a nest and keep their egg up off the ice on their feet instead. This is then covered with a fold of skin (called a brood patch) to keep the egg warm until it hatches, which can take up to 9 weeks to happen.

Penguins can easily drink sea water but have a special gland that removes the salt from their bodies. The salt is then pushed out through groves in their bill.

Penguins can talk to each other by waving their fins, bowing and calling out.

Penguins from New Zealand, Southern Australia and South Africa are smaller in size and have shorter feathers due to the warmer climates they live in.

While they may look friendly "Chinstrap" penguins are the most aggressive of all penguins.

Penguin's outer feathers are there to keep water out, while the inner down is used to trap air and keep the penguin warm in freezing water.

The deepest diving penguin on record is a female Emperor penguin which dived to a depth of 535m underwater.

A group of young penguins is called a "crèche".

Penguins can increase the blood flow to their flippers when they want to cool down. They can also pant like dogs and hold out their flippers to reduce their temperature.

World penguin day is the 25th of April.

Most penguins breed on exposed rocks except the Emperor penguin which can happily breed on ice floating in the sea.

Penguin eggs are smaller than other bird species when compared to the parent's body weight.

Penguins can stay under water for up to 15 minutes before coming up for air.

Penguins routinely leap from the water when swimming to catch small air bubbles. These air bubbles reduce friction and allow the penguin to swim faster. Leaping from the water is also used to avoid predators.

Penguins don't have teeth but use their beaks along with spines on the roof of their mouth and tongue to help grab onto food.

While the male Emperor penguin incubates its egg, the female penguin stays at sea for over 60 days to build up her fat reserves. She then returns to take care of and feed her newly hatched chick.

Penguins have more feathers than any other bird, In the case of the Emperor penguin it has 100 feathers per 1 square inch.

Emperor penguins only lay one egg compared to most other penguins that give birth to two.

Penguin's eye's work better underwater than above water.

Emperor penguins can happily live on floating ice all their lives and never set foot on land.

While incubating an egg an Emperor penguin can spend almost a full 24hrs asleep.

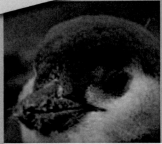

A group of penguins on land is called a "Waddle."

Penguins have a clear membrane on their eye called a "third eye lid" which protects their eyes from injury.

Penguins enter and leave the sea in large groups, for the reason that "There's safety in numbers". This helps to confuse and prevent any attacks from predators that may be swimming nearby.

A group of penguins in the water is called a "Raft."

Penguins are coloured black and white to protect them from predators. The white on their belly protects them from predators swimming below them in the sea, and the black protects them from predators seeing them from above.

Scientists can now follow and track penguins with the help of satellites without having to disturb them. Using powerful cameras they can track the penguins from the "poop" droppings they leave behind.

There are between 17 - 20 different types of penguins in the world, of that 10 are considered endangered.

Penguins don't normally fall over on their backs but when they do they can find it hard to get back up.

Unlike other birds, penguins moult and lose all their feathers in one go. Before this happens penguins must put on extra body weight (between 50-70%) and stay on land, until their new feathers grow back.

Gentoo penguins can swim at up to 35km an hour in the water.

Gentoo penguins can dive up to 150m underwater and in extreme cases have been known to dive for up to 15 hours non-stop (that's around 450 dives).

The rarest penguin in the world is the "Yellow Eyed" penguin with only 5000 still left in the world.

Blue penguins give birth to the smallest chicks weighing only 35grams at birth.

Penguins come with various different eye colors ranging from brown, yellow, bluish grey to even red.

Penguin nesting areas are called "Rookeries".

A penguin's normal body temperature is around 38° C.

Like whales, penguins have a layer of blubber that helps them to keep warm on land and sea. This is another reason why penguins have heavy bones, as blubber likes to float and penguin's bones counteract this problem.

And finally, fossils of penguins from up to 60 million years ago were a lot larger than our present penguins. One species was found to be almost as tall as a fully grown man.

When you get to the end of this book you'll be asked by your device to leave a comment or review...

# Penguins
## Facts About Penguins

A CHILDRENS WORLD BOOK COLLECTION

Could you please do so, it only takes a moment and it would help me to get my "Facts About Penguins" book in front of more new readers. Thank you for your help, Barry.

For More Great Childrens
Books Visit
www.SmartWordBooks.com

# Whales
## Facts About Whales

A CHILDRENS WORLD BOOK COLLECTION

BARRY J MCDONALD

# Sharks
## Facts About Sharks

A CHILDRENS WORLD BOOK COLLECTION

BARRY J MCDONALD

# Dinosaurs
## Facts About Dinosaurs

A CHILDRENS WORLD BOOK COLLECTION

BARRY J MCDONALD

16482382R00018

Made in the USA
Middletown, DE
15 December 2014